Society Massachusetts Historical

Tributes to Longfellow and Emerson

Society Massachusetts Historical

Tributes to Longfellow and Emerson

ISBN/EAN: 9783744677479

Printed in Europe, USA, Canada, Australia, Japan

Cover: Foto ©ninafisch / pixelio.de

More available books at **www.hansebooks.com**

TRIBUTES

TO

LONGFELLOW AND EMERSON

BY

The Massachusetts Historical Society.

HENRY WADSWORTH LONGFELLOW.

TRIBUTES

TO

LONGFELLOW AND EMERSON

BY

The Massachusetts Historical Society.

WITH PORTRAITS.

BOSTON:

A. WILLIAMS AND CO., PUBLISHERS,

OLD CORNER BOOKSTORE, 283 WASHINGTON ST.

1882.

Printed by permission of
THE MASSACHUSETTS HISTORICAL SOCIETY.

UNIVERSITY PRESS:
JOHN WILSON AND SON, CAMBRIDGE.

CONTENTS.

HENRY WADSWORTH LONGFELLOW.

BORN FEBRUARY 27, 1807.

DIED MARCH 24, 1882.

TRIBUTES TO LONGFELLOW.

THE monthly meeting of the Massachusetts Historical Society was held on Thursday, April 13, 1882. In the absence of Hon. Robert C. Winthrop, president of the society, who has recently sailed for Europe, the senior vice-president, Dr. George E. Ellis, occupied the chair. The librarian, Mayor Green, read the monthly list of donors to the library. Rev. E. G. Porter read a communication from the St. Botolph Club accepting Dr. Ellis's gift of a silver-gilt loving-cup, formerly belonging to the corporation of Boston, Lincolnshire, England, and now presented to the club upon the condition "that if ever the club shall be disbanded, or its assets dispersed, the cup shall revert to the Massachusetts Historical Society." The corresponding secretary, Mr. Winsor, read a letter from Professor J. R. Seeley of Cambridge, England, accepting the position of honorary membership in the society.

Vice-President ELLIS then said : —

REMARKS OF DR. ELLIS.

MUCH to our regret we miss our honored President from his chair to-day, on this, the ninety-first annual meeting of the Society. It is gratifying to be assured that he has

safely reached the other side of the ocean, and may be
looked for with us again early in the autumn. It will be
remembered that in opening the last meeting he expressed
for us all the relief which he found in not being called upon,
as in such rapid and melancholy succession he had been at
so many previous meetings, to announce a loss from our
limited roll of associates. But again must there be stricken
from it the name of one who leaves upon the list no other
so enshrined in the affection, the grateful homage, we may
even say the venerating regard of the world-wide fellowship of civilized humanity.

On the announcement to our deeply-moved community
of the death of Mr. Longfellow, though I had taken leave of
Mr. Winthrop near the eve of his departure, I wrote to him
asking that he would commit to me, to be read here and
now, what he would himself have said if he were to be with
us to-day. In his brief note of reply he writes, " How gladly
would I comply with your suggestion, and send you, for the
next meeting of our Society, some little tribute to our
lamented Longfellow. But at this last hurried moment
before leaving home, I could do justice neither to him nor
to myself. I was just going out to bid him good-by, when
his serious illness was announced, and in a day or two more
all was over. The last time he was in Europe I was there
with him, and I was a witness to not a few of the honors
which he received from high and low. I remember partic-
ularly that when we were coming away from the House of
Lords together, where we had been hearing a fine speech
from his friend the Duke of Argyll, a group of the common
people gathered around our carriage, calling him by name,

begging to touch his hand, and at least one of them reciting aloud one of his most familiar poems. No poet of our day has touched the common heart like Longfellow. The simplicity and purity of his style were a part of his own character. He had nothing of that irritability which is one of the proverbial elements of the poetic temperament, but was always genial, generous, lovely." . . . I will not attempt to add anything, as tribute, to that heart utterance from our President. Indeed, it would be difficult to find variations in the terms of language even, much more in the sentiments to be expressed by them, in tributes of tender and appreciative regard and affection for Mr. Longfellow. Full and profound in depth and earnestness have been the honors to him in speech and print; richer still, because unutterable, and only for the privacy of those who cherish them, are the responsive silences of the heart.

It is fitting, however, that we put on record our recognition of Mr. Longfellow in his relations to this Society. He accepted the membership to which he had been elected in December, 1857. Those who were associates in it twenty-five years ago will recall two signal occasions delightfully associated with his presence and speech. The one was a special meeting, to which he invited the Society at his own residence, as Washington's headquarters, in Cambridge, on June 17th, 1858. There was much of charming and instructive interest in the scenes and associations of the occasion, added to the communications made by several members full of historic information freshly related from original sources. The host himself was silent, save as by his genial greeting and warm hospitality he welcomed his grateful guests. The

other marked occasion was also at a special meeting of the
Society, held in December, 1859, at the house of our associate, Mr. Sears. The meeting was devoted to tributes of
respect and affection for Washington Irving, from many
who had shared his most intimate friendship. Mr. Longfellow gave hearty and delicate expression to his regard for
Irving, while Everett, Felton, Colonel Aspinwall, Prescott,
and Dr. Holmes contributed their offerings to the memory
of that admired author. But few of our associates, in its
nearly a century of years, can have studied our local and
even national history more sedulously than did Mr. Longfellow. And but fewer still among us can have found in its
stern and rugged and homely actors and annals so much
that could be graced and softened by rich and delicate
fancies, by refining sentiments, and the hues and fragrance
of simple poetry. He took the saddest of our New England tragedies, and the sweetest of its rural home scenes,
the wayside inn, the alarum of war, the Indian legend, and
the hanging of the crane in the modest household, and his
genius has invested them with enduring charms and morals.
Wise and gentle was the heart which could thus find melodies for the harp, the lyre, and the plectrum in our fields
and wildernesses, wreathing them as nature does the thickets
and stumps of the forest with flowers and mosses. While
all his utterances came from a pure, a tender, and a devout
heart, addressing themselves to what is of like in other
hearts, there is not in them a line of morbidness, of depres-
sion, or melancholy, but only that which quickens and
cheers with robust resolve and courage, with peace and
aspiring trust. He has, indeed, used freely the poet's

license in playful freedom with dates and facts. But the scenes and incidents and personages which most need a softening and refining touch, receive it from him without prejudice to the service of sober history.

The following resolution was then offered: —

Resolved, That in yielding from our roll the name of Henry Wadsworth Longfellow, we would put on our records the expression of our profoundest regard, esteem, and admiring appreciation of his character and genius, and our grateful sense of the honor and satisfaction we have shared in his companionship.

The resolution was seconded by Dr. OLIVER WENDELL HOLMES, who arose and addressed the Society with much feeling, as follows: —

REMARKS OF DR. HOLMES.

It is with no vain lamentations, but rather with profound gratitude that we follow the soul of our much-loved and long-loved poet beyond the confines of the world he helped so largely to make beautiful. We could have wished to keep him longer, but at least we were spared witnessing the inevitable shadows of an old age protracted too far beyond its natural limits. From the first notes of his fluent and harmonious song to the last, which comes to us as the "voice fell like a falling star," there has never been a discord. The music of the mountain stream, in the poem which reaches us from the other shore of being is as clear and sweet as the melodies of the youthful and middle periods of his minstrelsy. It has been a fully rounded life, beginning early with large promise, equalling every anticipation in its maturity, fertile and beautiful to its close in the ripeness of its well-filled years.

Until the silence fell upon us we did not entirely appreciate how largely his voice was repeated in the echoes of our own hearts. The affluence of his production so accustomed us to look for a poem from him at short intervals that we could hardly feel how precious that was which was so abundant. Not, of course, that every single poem reached the standard of the highest among them all. That could not be in Homer's time, and mortals must occasionally nod now as then. But the hand of the artist shows itself unmistakably in everything which left his desk. The O of Giotto could not help being a perfect round, and the verse of Longfellow is always perfect in construction.

He worked in that simple and natural way which characterizes the master. But it is one thing to be simple through poverty of intellect, and another thing to be simple by repression of all redundancy and overstatement; one thing to be natural through ignorance of all rules, and another to have made a second nature out of the sovereign rules of art. In respect of this simplicity and naturalness, his style is in strong contrast to that of many writers of our time. There is no straining for effect, there is no torturing of rhythm for novel patterns, no wearisome iteration of petted words, no inelegant clipping of syllables to meet the exigencies of a verse; no affected archaism, rarely any liberty taken with language, unless it may be in the form of a few words in the translation of Dante. I will not except from these remarks the singular and original form which he gave to his poem of " Hiawatha,"—a poem with a curious history in many respects. Suddenly and immensely popular in this country, greatly admired by many foreign critics, imitated with perfect ease by any clever schoolboy, serving as a model for metrical advertisements, made fun of, sneered at, abused, admired, but, at any rate, a picture full of pleasing fancies and melodious cadences. The very names are jewels which the most fastidious muse might be proud to wear. Coming from the realm of the Androscoggin and of Moosetukmaguntuk, how could he have found two such delicious names as Hiawatha and Minnehaha? The eight-syllable trochaic verse of " Hiawatha," like the eight-syllable iambic verse of " The Lady of the Lake," and others of Scott's poems, has a fatal facility, which I have elsewhere endeavored to explain on physiological principles. The recital of each line uses up the air of one natural expiration, so that we read, as we naturally do, eighteen or twenty lines in a minute, without disturbing the normal rhythm of breathing, which is also eighteen or twenty breaths to the minute. The standing objection to this is, that it makes the octo-syllabic verse too easy writing and too slipshod reading. Yet in this most frequently criticised composition the poet has shown a subtle sense of the requirements of his simple story of a primitive race, in choosing the most fluid of measures, that lets the thought run through it in easy sing-song, such as oral tradition would be sure to find on the lips of the story-tellers of the wigwam. Although Longfellow was not fond of metrical contortions and acrobatic achievements, he well knew the effects of skilful variation in the forms of verse and well-managed refrains or repetitions. In one of his very earliest poems, — " Pleasant it was when Woods were Green," — the dropping a syllable from the last line is an agreeable surprise to the ear, expecting only the common monotony of scrupulously balanced lines. In " Excelsior " the repetition of the aspiring exclamation which gives its name to the poem, lifts every stanza a step higher than the one which preceded it. In the " Old Clock on the Stair," the solemn words, " Forever, never, never, forever," give wonderful effectiveness to that most impressive poem.

All his art, all his learning, all his melody, cannot account for his extraordinary popularity, not only among his own countrymen and those who in other lands speak the language in which he wrote, but in foreign realms, where he could only be read through the ground glass of a translation. It was in his choice of subjects that one source of the public favor with which his writings, more especially his poems, were received, obviously lay. A poem, to be widely popular, must deal with thoughts and emotions that belong to common, not exceptional character, conditions, interests. The most popular of all books are those which meet the spiritual needs of mankind most powerfully, such works as " The Imitation of Christ " and " Pilgrim's Progress." I suppose if the great multitude of readers were to render a decision as to which of Longfellow's poems they most valued, the " Psalm of Life " would command the largest number. This is a brief homily enforcing the great truths of duty, and of our relation to the unseen world. Next in order would very probably come " Excelsior," a poem that springs up-

ward like a flame and carries the soul up with it in its
aspiration for the unattainable ideal. If this sounds like a
trumpet-call to the fiery energies of youth, not less does the
still small voice of that most sweet and tender poem, "Resignation," appeal to the sensibilities of those who have lived
long enough to have known the bitterness of such a be-
reavement as that out of which grew the poem. Or take a
poem before referred to, " The Old Clock on the Stair,"
and in it we find the history of innumerable households told
in relating the history of one, and the solemn burden of the
song repeats itself to thousands of listening readers, as if
the beat of the pendulum were throbbing at the head of
every staircase. Such poems as these — and there are many
more of not unlike character — are the foundation of that
universal acceptance his writings obtain among all classes.
But for these appeals to universal sentiment, his readers
would have been confined to a comparatively small circle of
educated and refined readers. There are thousands and
tens of thousands who are familiar with what we might call
his household poems, who have never read the "Spanish
Student," " The Golden Legend," " Hiawatha," or even
" Evangeline." Again, ask the first schoolboy you meet
which of Longfellow's poems he likes best, and he will be
very likely to answer, " Paul Revere's Ride." When he is a
few years older he might perhaps say, " The Building of the
Ship," that admirably constructed poem, beginning with the
literal description, passing into the higher region of sentiment by the most natural of transitions, and ending with
the noble climax, —

" Thou, too, sail on, O ship of state,"

3

which has become the classical expression of patriotic emotion.

Nothing lasts like a coin and a lyric. Long after the dwellings of men have disappeared, when their temples are in ruins and all their works of art are shattered, the ploughman strikes an earthen vessel holding the golden and silver disks, on which the features of a dead monarch, with emblems it may be, betraying the beliefs or the manners, the rudeness or the finish of art and all which this implies, survive an extinct civilization. Pope has expressed this with his usual Horatian felicity, in the letter to Addison, on the publication of his little " Treatise on Coins," —

> " A small Euphrates through the piece is rolled,
> And little eagles wave their wings in gold."

Conquerors and conquered sink in common oblivion ; triumphal arches, pageants the world wonders at, all that trumpeted itself as destined to an earthly immortality pass away; the victor of a hundred battles is dust; the parchments or papyrus on which his deeds were written are shrivelled and decayed and gone, —

> "And all his triumphs shrink into a coin."

So it is with a lyric poem. One happy utterance of some emotion or expression, which comes home to all, may keep a name remembered when the race to which the singer belonged is lost sight of. The cradle-song of Danaë to her infant as they tossed on the waves in the imprisoning chest, has made the name of Simonides immortal. Our own English literature abounds with instances which illustrate the same fact so far as the experience of a few generations extends.

And I think we may venture to say that some of the shorter
poems of Longfellow must surely reach a remote posterity,
and be considered then, as now, ornaments to English literature. We may compare them with the best short poems
of the language without fearing that they will suffer. Scott,
cheerful, wholesome, unreflective, should be read in the
open air; Byron, the poet of malcontents and cynics, in a
prison cell; Burns, generous, impassioned, manly, social, in
the tavern hall; Moore, elegant, fastidious, full of melody,
scented with the volatile perfume of the Eastern gardens, in
which his fancy revelled, is pre-eminently the poet of the
drawing-room and the piano; Longfellow, thoughtful, musical, home-loving, busy with the lessons of life, which he was
ever studying, and loved to teach others, finds his charmed
circle of listeners by the fireside. His songs, which we
might almost call sacred ones, rarely if ever get into the
hymn-books. They are too broadly human to suit the
specialized tastes of the sects, which often think more of their
differences from each other than of the common ground on
which they can agree. Shall we think less of our poet
because he so frequently aimed in his verse not simply to
please, but also to impress some elevating thought on the
minds of his readers? The Psalms of King David are burn-
ing with religious devotion and full of weighty counsel, but
they are not less valued, certainly, than the poems of Omar
Khayam, which cannot be accused of too great a tendency
to find a useful lesson in their subject. Dennis, the famous
critic, found fault with the "Rape of the Lock" because it
had no moral. It is not necessary that a poem should carry
a moral, any more than that a picture of a Madonna should

always be an altar-piece. The poet himself is the best
judge of that in each particular case. In that charming
little poem of Wordsworth's, ending, —

> "And then my heart with rapture thrills
> And dances with the daffodils,"

we do not ask for anything more than the record of the
impression which is told so simply, and which justifies itself
by the way in which it is told. But who does not feel
with the poet that the touching story, "Hartleap Well,"
must have its lesson brought out distinctly, to give a fitting
close to the narrative? Who would omit those two lines?—

> "Never to blend our pleasure or our pride
> With sorrow of the meanest thing that lives."

No poet knew better than Longfellow how to impress a
moral without seeming to preach. Didactic verse, as such,
is, no doubt, a formidable visitation, but a cathedral has its
lesson to teach as well as a schoolhouse. These beautiful
medallions of verse which Longfellow has left us might
possibly be found fault with as conveying too much useful
and elevating truth in their legends; having the unartistic
aim of being serviceable as well as delighting by their
beauty. Let us leave such comment to the critics who
cannot handle a golden coin, fresh from the royal mint,
without clipping its edges and stamping their own initials
on its face.

Of the longer poems of our chief singer, I should not
hesitate to select "Evangeline" as the masterpiece, and I
think the general verdict of opinion would confirm my
choice. The German model which it follows in its measure

and the character of its story was itself suggested by an earlier idyl. If Dorothea was the mother of Evangeline, Luise was the mother of Dorothea. And what a beautiful creation is the Acadian maiden! From the first line of the poem, from its first words, we read as we would float down a broad and placid river, murmuring softly against its banks, heaven over it and the glory of the unspoiled wilderness all around,

"This is the forest primeval."

The words are already as familiar as

"Μῆνιν ἄειδε, θεά,"

or

"Arma virumque cano."

The hexameter has been often criticised, but I do not believe any other measure could have told that lovely story with such effect, as we feel when carried along the tranquil current of these brimming, slow-moving, soul-satisfying lines. Imagine for one moment a story like this minced into octosyllabics. The poet knows better than his critics the length of step which best befits his muse.

I will not take up your time with any further remarks upon writings so well known to all. By the poem I have last mentioned, and by his lyrics, or shorter poems, I think the name of Longfellow will be longest remembered. Whatever he wrote, whether in prose or poetry, bore always the marks of the finest scholarship, the purest taste, fertile imagination, a sense of the music of words, and a skill in bringing it out of our English tongue, which hardly more than one of his contemporaries who write in that language can be said to equal.

The saying of Buffon, that the style is the man himself, or of the man himself, as some versions have it, was never truer than in the case of our beloved poet. Let us understand by style all that gives individuality to the expression of a writer; and in the subjects, the handling, the spirit and aim of his poems, we see the reflex of a personal character which made him worthy of that almost unparalleled homage which crowned his noble life. Such a funeral procession as attended him in thought to his resting-place has never joined the train of mourners that followed the hearse of a poet, — could we not say of any private citizen ? And we all feel that no tribute could be too generous, too universal, to the union of a divine gift with one of the loveliest of human characters.

Dr. Holmes was followed by Professor Charles Eliot Norton, who arose and said, —

REMARKS OF PROFESSOR NORTON.

I could wish that this were a silent meeting. There is no need of formal commemorative speech to-day, for all the people of the land, the whole English-speaking race, — and not they alone, — mourn our friend and poet. Never was poet so mourned, for never was poet so beloved.

There is nothing of lamentation in our mourning. He has not been untimely taken. His life was " prolonged with many years, happy and famous." Death came to him in good season, or ever the golden bowl was broken, or the pitcher broken at the cistern. Desire had but lately failed.

Life was fair to him almost to its end. On his seventy-fourth birthday, a little more than a year ago, with his family and a few friends round his dinner table, he said, "There seems to me a mistake in the order of the years: I can hardly believe that the four should not precede the seven." But in the year that followed he experienced the pains and languor and weariness of age. There was no complaint — the sweetness of his nature was invincible.

On one of the last times that I saw him, as I entered his familiar study on a beautiful afternoon of this past winter, I said to him, "I hope this is a good day for you?" He replied, with a pleasant smile, "Ah! there are no good days now." Happily, the evil days were not to be many. . . .

The accord between the character and life of Mr. Longfellow and his poems was complete. His poetry touched the hearts of his readers because it was the sincere expression of his own. The sweetness, the gentleness, the grace, the purity of his verse were the image of his own soul. But beautiful and ample as this expression of himself was, it fell short of the truth. The man was more and better than the poet.

Intimate, however, as was the concord between the poet and his poetry, there was much in him to which he never gave utterance in words. He was a man of deep reserves. He kept the holy of holies within himself inviolable and secluded. Seldom does he admit his readers to even its outward precincts. The deepest experiences of life are too sacred to be shared with any one whatsoever. "There are things of which I may not speak," he says in one of the most personal of his poems.

"Whose hand shall dare to open and explore
Those volumes closed and clasped forevermore?
Not mine. With reverential feet I pass."

.   .   .   .

It was the felicity of Mr. Longfellow to share the sentiment and emotion of his coevals, and to succeed in giving
to them their apt poetic expression. It was not by depth
of thought or by original views of nature that he won his
place in the world's regard; but it was by sympathy with
the feelings common to good men and women everywhere,
and by the simple, direct, sincere, and delicate expression
of them, that he gained the affection of mankind.

He was fortunate in the time of his birth. He grew up
in the morning of our republic. He shared in the cheer-
fulness of the early hour, in its hopefulness, its confidence.
The years of his youth and early manhood coincided with
an exceptional moment of national life, in which a prosperous and unembarrassed democracy was learning its own
capacities, and was beginning to realize its large and novel
resources; in which the order of society was still simple
and humane. He became, more than any one else, the
voice of this epoch of national progress, an epoch of unex-
ampled prosperity for the masses of mankind in our new
world, prosperity from which sprang a sense, more general
and deeper than had ever before been felt, of human kind-
ness and brotherhood. But, even to the prosperous, life
brings its inevitable burden. Trial, sorrow, misfortune, are
not to be escaped by the happiest of men. The deepest
experiences of each individual are the experiences common
to the whole race. And it is this double aspect of American
life — its novel and happy conditions, with the genial spirit

resulting from them, and, at the same time, its subjection to the old, absolute, universal laws of existence — that finds its mirror and manifestation in Longfellow's poetry.

No one can read his poetry without a conviction of the simplicity, tenderness, and humanity of the poet. And we who were his friends know how these qualities shone in his daily conversation. Praise, applause, flattery, — and no man ever was exposed to more of them, — never touched him to harm him. He walked through their flames un-scathed, as Dante through the fires of purgatory. His modesty was perfect. He accepted the praise as he would have accepted any other pleasant gift, — glad of it as an expression of good will, but without personal elation. In-deed, he had too much of it, and often in an absurd form, not to become at times weary of what his own fame and virtues brought upon him. But his kindliness did not permit him to show his weariness to those who did but burden him with their admiration. It was the penalty of his genius, and he accepted it with the pleasantest temper and a humorous resignation. Bores of all nations, espe-cially of our own, persecuted him. His long-suffering pa-tience was a wonder to his friends. It was, in truth, the sweetest charity. No man was ever before so kind to these moral mendicants. One day I ventured to remonstrate with him on his endurance of the persecutions of one of the worst of the class, who to lack of modesty added lack of honesty, — a wretched creature, — and when I had done, he looked at me with a pleasant, reproving, humorous glance, and said, "Charles, who would be kind to him if I were not?" It was enough. He was helped by a gift of humor,

which, though seldom displayed in his poems, lighted up his
talk and added a charm to his intercourse. He was the
most gracious of men in his own home; he was fond of
the society of his friends, and the company that gathered
in his study or round his table took its tone from his own
genial, liberal, cultivated, and refined nature.

> "With loving breath of all the winds his name
>   Is blown about the world; but to his friends
> A sweeter secret hides behind his fame,
>   And love steals shyly through the loud acclaim
> To murmur a *God bless you!* and there ends."

His verse, his fame, are henceforth the precious posses-
sions of the people whom he loved so well. They will
be among the effective instruments in shaping the future
character of the nation. His spirit will continue to soften,
to refine, to elevate the hearts of men. He will be the
beloved friend of future generations as he has been of his
own. His desire will be gratified, —

> "And in your life let my remembrance linger,
>   As something not to trouble and disturb it,
> But to complete it, adding life to life.
> And if at times beside the evening fire
> You see my face among the other faces,
> Let it not be regarded as a ghost
> That haunts your house, but as a guest that loves you,
> Nay, even as one of your own family,
> Without whose presence there were something wanting.
> I have no more to say."

Mr. WILLIAM EVERETT spoke with much force of the pre-
eminent gifts of Mr. Longfellow, and, although not given to

comparisons, he could not help putting his "Ship of State" alongside of Horace's passionate burst of song beginning "O navis!" After reciting the two, Mr. Everett declared that our singer had encountered the greatest lyric poet of Rome on his own ground, and, grappling with him, had fairly thrown him.

The resolution was unanimously adopted by a standing vote.

RALPH WALDO EMERSON.

PHOTOGRAPHED IN 1857 BY J. J. HAWES, BOSTON.

RALPH WALDO EMERSON.

BORN MAY 25, 1803.

DIED APRIL 27, 1882.

TRIBUTES TO EMERSON.

The regular monthly meeting of the Massachusetts Historical Society was held on Thursday, May 11, 1882, at three o'clock, P.M. In the absence of the president, the Hon. Robert C. Winthrop, who is spending the summer in Europe, the senior vice-president, George E. Ellis, D.D., occupied the chair. The minutes of the April meeting, at which tributes were paid to Mr. Longfellow, were read by the Rev. E. G. Porter, recording secretary *pro tem*. The librarian, Mayor Green, read the monthly list of donors to the Library. The corresponding secretary, Mr. Justin Winsor, made his report, after which Vice-President ELLIS gave the following address: —

REMARKS OF DR. ELLIS.

MANY of us who meet in this library to-day are doubtless recalling vividly the memory of the impressive scene here when, fifteen months ago, Mr. Emerson, appearing among us for the last time, read his characteristic paper upon Thomas Carlyle. It was the very hour on which the remains of that remarkable man were committed to his Scotch grave. There was much to give the occasion here a deep and tender interest. We could not but feel that it

was the last utterance to which we should listen from our
beloved and venerated associate, if not, as it proved to be,
the last of his presence among us.   So we listened greedily
and fondly.   The paper had been lying in manuscript more
than thirty years, but it had kept its freshness and fidelity.
The matter of it, its tone and utterance, were singularly
suggestive.   Not the least of the crowding reflections with
which we listened was the puzzling wonder, to some of us,
as to the tie of sympathy and warm personal attachment,
of nearly half a century's continuance, between the serene
and gentle spirit of our poet-philosopher and the stormy
and aggressive spirit of Mr. Carlyle.

There are those immediately to follow me who, with acute
and appreciative minds, in closeness of intercourse and sympathy with Mr. Emerson, will interpret to you the form and
significance of his genius, the richness of his fine and rare
endowments, and account to you for the admiring and loving
estimate of his power and influence and world-wide fame
in the lofty realms of thought, with insight and vision and
revealings of the central mysteries of being.   They must
share largely in those rare gifts of his who undertake to be
the channel of them from him to others.   For it is no secret,
but a free confession, that the quality, methods, and fruits of
his genius are so peculiar, unique, obscure, and remote from
the appreciation of a large class of those of logical, argu-
mentative, and prosaic minds, as to invest them with the
ill-understood and the inexplicable.   He was signally one
of those, rare in our race, in the duality of our human ele-
mentary composition, in whom the dust of the ground contributed its least proportion, while the ethereal inspiration
from above contributed the greatest.

The words which I would add, prompted as in keeping with this place and occasion, shall be in reminiscence of years long past. Those whose memories are clear and strong, and who forty-five years ago in their professional, literary, or social fellowships were intent upon all that quickened thought and converse in this peculiar centre of Boston and its neighborhoods, will recall with what can hardly be other than pensive retrospects the charms and fervors, the surprises, and perhaps the shocks, certainly the bewilderment and the apprehension, which signalled the· announcement here of what was called Transcendentalism. Though the word was from the first wrongfully applied, there was an aptness in its use, as in keeping with the mistiness and cloudiness of the dispensation to which it was attached. The excitement here was adjusted to the size, the composition, the tone and spirit, and the unassimilated elements of this community. The movement had the quickening zest of mystery. It was long before those who were not a part of it could reach to any intelligible idea of what it might signify, or promise, or portend. There were a score, a hundred, persons craving to have explained to them what it all meant, to each one who seemed ready or able in volunteering to throw light upon it. And this intended light was often but an adumbration. Mr. Emerson gained nothing from his interpreters. Nor does he now. The key which they offered did not fit the wards of the lock. The vagueness of the oracle seemed to be deepened when repeated by any other lips than those which gave it first utterance. In most of the recent references in the news-papers and magazines to the opening of Mr. Emerson's

career in high philosophy, emphatic statements are made
as to the ridicule and satire and banter evoked by the first
utterances of this transcendentalism. It is not impressed
upon my memory that any of this triviality was ever spent
upon Mr. Emerson himself. The modest, serene, unaggres-
sive attitude, and personal phenomena of bearing and utterance which were so winningly characteristic of his presence
and speech, as he dropped the sparkles and nuggets of his
fragmentary revelations, were his ample security against all
such disrespect. The fun, as I remember, was spent upon
the first circle of repeaters, and so-called disciples, a small
but lively company of both sexes, who seemed to patent
him as their oracle, as an inner fellowship who would be
the medium between him and the unillumined. Nor was
it strange that explanations, or demonstrative and argu-
mentative expositions of the Emersonian philosophy prof-
fered by its interpreters did not open it clearly to inquirers,
inasmuch as he himself assured us that it was not to be
learned or tested by old-fashioned familiar methods. I
know of but one piece from his pen now in print, and
dating from the first year of his publicity, in which he
appears, not in self-defence under challenge, — for he never
did that, — but in attempted and baffled self-exposition.
Nor have lines ever been written, by himself or by his
interpreters, so apt, so characteristic, so exquisitely phrased
and toned, so exhaustively descriptive of the style and
spirit of his philosophy as those which I will quote.

The younger Henry Ware, whose colleague he had been
during his brief pastorship of a church, disturbed by something in a discourse which Mr. Emerson, after leaving the

pulpit, had delivered in Cambridge in 1838, had preached in
the College chapel a sermon dealing in part with a position
which had startled himself and others in his friend's address,
and, in part, with a breeze of excitement which it had raised
in a tinderish community. The sermon being printed, Mr.
Ware sent a copy of it to Mr. Emerson, with a letter, which
the latter says "was right manly and noble." The letter
expressed a little disturbance, puzzle, and anxiety of mind,
and put some questions hinting at desired explanations and
arguments.

In reply Mr Emerson interprets himself thus: —

"If the sermon assails any doctrines of mine, — perhaps
I am not so quick to see it as writers generally, — certainly
I did not feel any disposition to depart from my habitual
contentment, that you should say your thought whilst I
say mine. I believe I must tell you what I think of my
new position. It strikes me very oddly that good and wise
men at Cambridge and Boston should think of raising me
into an object of criticism. I have always been — from my
very incapacity of methodical writing — 'a chartered liber-
tine,' free to worship and free to rail, lucky when I could
make myself understood, but never esteemed near enough
to the institutions and mind of society to deserve the notice
of the masters of literature and religion. I have appre-
ciated fully the advantages of my position, for I well know
that there is no scholar less able or willing to be a polemic.
I could not give accounts of myself if challenged. I could
not possibly give you one of the 'arguments' you cruelly
hint at, on which any doctrine of mine stands. For I do not
know what arguments mean, in reference to any expression

of a thought. I delight in telling what I think; but, if you ask me how I dare say so, or why it is so, I am the most helpless of mortal men. I do not even see that either of these questions admits of an answer. So that in the present droll posture of my affairs, when I see myself suddenly raised into the importance of a heretic, I am very uneasy when I advert to the supposed duties of such a personage, who is to make good his thesis against all comers. I certainly shall do no such thing. I shall read what you and other good men write, as I have always done, — glad when you speak my thoughts, and skipping the page that has nothing for me. I shall go on, just as before, seeing whatever I can, and telling what I see; and, I suppose, with the same fortune that has hitherto attended me, — the joy of finding that my abler and better brothers, who work with the sympathy of society, loving and beloved, do now and then unexpectedly confirm my perceptions, and find my nonsense is only their own thought in motley."

No one in comment, essay, or criticism upon Mr. Emerson has improved upon his own revealing of his philosophy of intuition, insight, eye, and thought, as distinguished from that of logic and argument. It needed some considerable lapse of time, with much wondering, questioning, and debating in this community, to clear the understanding, that the new and hopeful message brought to us was something like this, — that those who were overfed, or starved, or wearied with didactic, prosaic lessons of truth for life and conduct, through formal teaching, by reasoning, arguings and provings, might turn to their own inner furnishings, to their thinkings as processes, not results, and to the free revealings and inspirings from without as interpreted from within.

But whatever was the baffling secret of Mr. Emerson's philosophy, there was no mystery save that to the charm and power of which we all love to yield ourselves, in the poise and repose of his placid spirit, in the grace and felicity of his utterance, in the crowding of sense and suggestiveness into his short, terse sentences, in his high reachings for all truth as its disciple, and in the persuasiveness with which he communicated to others what was disclosed to him. He never answered to a challenge by apology or controversy.

At the conclusion of his address, Dr. Ellis read the following letter from Judge HOAR : —

LETTER OF THE HON. E. R. HOAR.

CONCORD, May 8, 1882.

MY DEAR DR. ELLIS, — I find that it will be out of my power to attend the meeting of the Historical Society on Thursday next, and I am sorry to lose the opportunity of hearing the tributes which its members will pay to the memory of Mr. Emerson, than whose name none more worthy of honor is found on its roll. His place in literature, as poet, philosopher, seer, and thinker, will find much more adequate statement than any which I could offer. But there are two things which the Proceedings of our Society may appropriately record concerning him, one of them likely to be lost sight of in the lustre of his later and more famous achievements, and the other of a quality so evanescent as to be preserved only by contemporary evidence and tradition.

The first relates to his address in September, 1835, at the celebration of the two hundredth anniversary of the settlement of Concord; which seems to me to contain the most complete and exquisite picture of the origin, history, and peculiar characteristics of a New England town that has ever been produced.

The second is his *power as an orator*, rare and peculiar, and in its way unequalled among our cotemporaries.   Many of us can recall instances of it, and there are several prominent in my recollection; but perhaps the most striking was his address at the Burns centennial, in Boston, on the 25th of January, 1859.

The company that he addressed was a queer mixture. First, there were the Burns club, — grave, critical, and long-headed Scotchmen, jealous of the fame of their countryman, and doubtful of the capacity to appreciate him in men of other blood.   There were the scholars and poets of Boston and its neighborhood, and professors and undergraduates from Harvard College.   Then there were state and city officials, aldermen and common councilmen, brokers and bank directors, ministers and deacons, doctors, lawyers, and "carnal self-seekers" of every grade.

I have had the good fortune to hear many of the chief orators of our time, among them Henry Clay, John Quincy Adams, Ogden Hoffman, S. S. Prentiss, William H. Seward, Charles Sumner, Wendell Phillips, George William Curtis, some of the great preachers, and Webster, Everett, Choate, and Winthrop at their best.   But I never witnessed such an effort of speech upon men as Mr. Emerson apparently then attained. It reached at once to his own definition of eloquence, — "a taking sovereign possession of the audience." He had uttered but a few sentences before he seemed to have welded together the whole mass of discordant material and lifted them to the same height of sympathy and passion. He excited them to smiles, to tears, to the wildest enthu-siasm. His tribute to Burns is beautiful to read, perhaps the best which the occasion produced on either side of the ocean. But the clear articulation, the ringing emphasis, the musical modulation of tone and voice, the loftiness of bearing, and the radiance of his face, all made a part of the consummate charm. When he closed, the company could hardly tolerate any other speaker, though good ones were to follow.

I am confident that every one who was present on that evening would agree with me as to the splendor of that eloquence.

Very truly yours,

E. R. Hoar.

Rev. George E. Ellis, D.D.,
 Vice-President of the Massachusetts Historical Society.

Dr. Oliver Wendell Holmes then arose and addressed the Society as follows : —

ADDRESS OF DR. HOLMES.

It is a privilege which any of us may claim, as we pass each of these last and newly raised mounds, to throw our pebble upon the cairn. For our own sakes we must be indulged in the gratification of paying our slender tribute.

So soon, alas, after bidding farewell to our cherished poet
to lose the earthly presence of the loftiest, the divinest of
our thinkers! The language of eulogy seemed to have
exhausted itself in celebrating him who was the darling
of two English worlds, the singer of Acadian and Pilgrim
and Indian story, of human affections and aspirations, of
sweet, wholesome life from its lullaby to its requiem. And
now we hardly know what measure to observe in our praises
of him who was singularly averse to over-statement, who
never listened approvingly to flattery when living, and whose
memory asks only the white roses of truth for its funeral
garlands.

The work of his life is before us all, and will have full
justice done it by those who are worthy of the task and
equal to its demands. But, as out of a score of photo-
graphs each gives us something of a friend's familiar face,
though all taken together do not give us the whole of it,
so each glimpse of reminiscence, each hint of momentary
impression, may help to make a portrait which shall remind
us of the original, though it is, at best, but an imperfect
resemblance.

When a life so exceptional as that which has just left our
earthly companionship appears in any group of our fellow-
creatures, we naturally ask how such a well-recognized supe-
riority came into being. We look for the reason of such
an existence among its antecedents, some of which we can
reach, as, for instance, the characteristics of the race, the
tribe, the family. The forces of innumerable generations
are represented in the individual, more especially those of
the last century or two. Involved with these, inextricable,

insoluble, is the mystery of mysteries, the mechanism of
personality. No such personality as this which was lately
present with us is the outcome of cheap paternity and
shallow motherhood.

I may seem to utter an Hibernian absurdity; I may
recall a lively couplet which has often brought a smile at
the expense of our good city; I may — I hope I shall not
— offend the guardians of ancient formulæ, vigilant still
as watch-dogs over the bones of their fleshless symbols,
but I must be permitted to say that I believe the second
birth may precede that which we consider as the first. The
divine renovation which changes the half-human animal,
the cave-dweller, the cannibal, into the servant of God, the
friend, the benefactor, the lawgiver of his kind, may, I
believe, be wrought in the race before it is incarnated in
the individual. It may take many generations of chosen
births to work the transformation, but what the old chem-
ists called *cohobation* is not without its meaning for vital
chemistry; life must pass through an alembic of gold or of
silver many times before its current can possibly run quite
clear.

A New Englander has a right to feel happy, if not proud,
if he can quarter his coat-of-arms with the bands of an
ancestry of clergymen. Eight generations of ministers
preceded the advent of this prophet of our time. There
is no better flint to strike fire from than the old nodule
of Puritanism. Strike it against the steel of self-asserting
civil freedom, and we get a flash and a flame such as showed
our three-hilled town to the lovers of liberty all over the
world. An ancestry of ministers, softened out of their old-

world dogmas by the same influences which set free the
colonies, is the true Brahminism of New England.

Children of the same parentage, as we well know, do not
alike manifest the best qualities belonging to the race.   But
those of the two brothers of Ralph Waldo Emerson whom
I can remember were of exceptional and superior natural
endowments.   Edward, next to him in order of birth, was
of the highest promise, only one evidence of which was his
standing at the head of his college class at graduation.   I
recall a tender and most impressive tribute of Mr. Everett's
to his memory, at one of our annual Phi Beta Kappa meetings.   He spoke of the blow which had jarred the strings
of his fine intellect and made them return a sound

" Like sweet bells jangled out of tune and harsh,"

in the saddened tones of that rich sonorous voice still thrill-
ing in the ears of many whose hearing is dulled for all the
music, all the eloquence of to-day.

Of Charles Chauncy, the youngest brother, I knew something in my college days.   A beautiful, high-souled, pure,
exquisitely delicate nature in a slight but finely wrought
mortal frame, he was for me the very ideal of an embodied
celestial intelligence.   I may venture to mention a trivial
circumstance, because it points to the character of his
favorite reading, which was likely to be guided by the
same tastes as his brother's, and may have been specially
directed by him.   Coming into my room one day, he took
up a copy of Hazlitt's British Poets.   He opened it to the
poem of Andrew Marvell's, entitled " The Nymph Com-
plaining for the Death of her Fawn," which he read to

me with delight irradiating his expressive features. The lines remained with me, or many of them, from that hour, —

> " Had it lived long, it would have been
> Lilies without, roses within."

I felt as many have felt after being with his brother, Ralph Waldo, that I had entertained an angel visitant. The Fawn of Marvell's imagination survives in my memory as the fitting image to recall this beautiful youth; a soul glowing like the rose of morning with enthusiasm, a character white as the lilies in its purity.

Such was the family nature lived out to its full development in Ralph Waldo Emerson. Add to this the special differentiating quality, indefinable as the tone of a voice, which we should know not the less, from that of every other of articulately speaking mortals, and we have the Emerson of our recollections.

A person who by force of natural gifts is entitled to be called a personage is always a surprise in the order of appearances, sometimes, as in the case of Shakespeare, of Goethe, a marvel, if not a miracle. The new phenomenon has to be studied like the young growth that sprang up between the stones in the story of Picciola. Is it a common weed, or a plant with virtues and beauties of its own? Is it a cryptogam that can never flower, or shall we wait and see it blossom by and by? Is it an endogen or an exogen, — did the seed it springs from drop from a neighboring bough, or was it wafted hither on the wings of the wind from some far-off shore?

Time taught us what to make of this human growth. It was not an annual or a biennial, but a perennial; not an herbaceous plant, but a towering tree; not an oak or an elm like those around it, but rather a lofty and spreading palm, which acclimated itself out of its latitude, as the little group of Southern magnolias has done in the woods of our northern county of Essex. For Emerson's was an Asiatic mind, drawing its sustenance partly from the hard soil of our New England, partly, too, from the air that has known Himalaya and the Ganges. So impressed with this character of his mind was Mr. Burlingame, as I saw him, after his return from his mission, that he said to me, in a freshet of hyperbole, which was the overflow of a channel with a thread of truth running in it, " There are twenty thousand Ralph Waldo Emersons in China."

What could we do with this unexpected, unprovided for, unclassified, half unwelcome new-comer, who had been for a while potted, as it were, in our Unitarian cold greenhouse, but had taken to growing so fast that he was lifting off its glass roof and letting in the hailstorms? Here was a protest that outflanked the extreme left of liberalism, yet so calm and serene that its radicalism had the accents of the gospel of peace. Here was an iconoclast without a hammer, who took down our idols from their pedestals so tenderly that it seemed like an act of worship.

The scribes and pharisees made light of his oracular sayings. The lawyers could not find the witnesses to subpœna and the documents to refer to when his case came before them, and turned him over to their wives and daughters. The ministers denounced his heresies, and handled his writings as if they were packages of dynamite, and the grandmothers were as much afraid of his new teachings as old

Mrs. Piozzi was of geology. We had had revolutionary orators, reformers, martyrs ; it was but a few years since Abner
Kneeland had been sent to jail for expressing an opinion
about the great First Cause ; but we had had nothing like
this man, with his seraphic voice and countenance, his
choice vocabulary, his refined utterance, his gentle courage,
which, with a different manner, might have been called
audacity, his temperate statement of opinions which
threatened to shake the existing order of thought like an
earthquake.

His peculiarities of style and of thinking became fertile
parents of mannerisms, which were fair game for ridicule
as they appeared in his imitators. For one who talks like
Emerson or like Carlyle soon finds himself surrounded by a
crowd of walking phonographs, who mechanically repro-
duce his mental and vocal accents. Emerson was before
long talking in the midst of a babbling Simonetta of echoes,
and not unnaturally was now and then himself a mark for
the small shot of criticism. He had soon reached that
height in the "cold thin atmosphere" of thought where

> Vainly the fowler's eye
> Might mark his distant flight to do him wrong.

I shall add a few words, of necessity almost epigram-
matic, upon his work and character. He dealt with life, and
life with him was not merely this particular air-breathing
phase of being, but the spiritual existence which included it
like a parenthesis between the two infinities. He wanted
his daily draughts of oxygen like his neighbors, and was as
thoroughly human as the plain people he mentions who had
successively owned or thought they owned the house-lot on

which he planted his hearthstone.   But he was at home no
less in the interstellar spaces outside of all the atmospheres.
The semi-materialistic idealism of Milton was a gross and
clumsy medium compared to the imponderable ether of
" The Oversoul " and the unimaginable vacuum of " Brah-
ma."   He followed in the shining and daring track of the
Graius homo of Lucretius :

> " Vivida vis animi pervicit, et extra
> Processit longe flammantia mœnia mundi."

It always seemed to me as if he looked at this earth very
much as a visitor from another planet would look upon it.
He was interested, and to some extent curious about it,
but it was not the first spheroid he had been acquainted
with, by any means.   I have amused myself with comparing
his descriptions of natural objects with those of the Angel
Raphael in the seventh book of Paradise Lost.   Emerson
talks of his titmouse as Raphael talks of his emmet.   An-
gels and poets never deal with nature after the manner of
those whom we call naturalists.

To judge of him as a thinker, Emerson should have been
heard as a lecturer, for his manner was an illustration of his
way of thinking.   He would lose his place just as his mind
would drop its thought and pick up another, twentieth
cousin or no relation at all to it.   This went so far at times
that one could hardly tell whether he was putting together
a mosaic of colored fragments, or only turning a kaleido-
scope where the pieces tumbled about as they best might.
It was as if he had been looking in at a cosmic peep-show,
and turning from it at brief intervals to tell us what he
saw.   But what fragments these colored sentences were,

and what pictures they often placed before us, as if we too saw them! Never has this city known such audiences as he gathered; never was such an Olympian entertainment as that which he gave them.

It is very hard to speak of Mr. Emerson's poetry; not to do it injustice, still more to do it justice. It seems to me like the robe of a monarch patched by a New England housewife. The royal tint and stuff are unmistakable, but here and there the gray worsted from the darning-needle crosses and ekes out the Tyrian purple. Few poets who have written so little in verse have dropped so many of those "jewels five words long" which fall from their setting only to be more choicely treasured. *E pluribus unum* is hardly more familiar to our ears than "He builded better than he knew," and Keats's "thing of beauty" is little better known than Emerson's "beauty is its own excuse for being." One may not like to read Emerson's poetry because it is sometimes careless, almost as if carefully so, though never undignified even when slipshod; spotted with quaint archaisms and strange expressions that sound like the affectation of negligence, or with plain, homely phrases, such as the self-made scholar is always afraid of. But if one likes Emerson's poetry he will be sure to love it; if he loves it, its phrases will cling to him as hardly any others do. It may not be for the multitude, but it finds its place like pollen-dust and penetrates to the consciousness it is to fertilize and bring to flower and fruit.

I have known something of Emerson as a talker, not nearly so much as many others who can speak and write of him. It is unsafe to tell how a great thinker talks, for per-

haps, like a city dealer with a village customer, he has not
shown his best goods to the innocent reporter of his sayings.   However that may be in this case, let me contrast in
a single glance the momentary effect in conversation of the
two neighbors, Hawthorne and Emerson.   Speech seemed
like a kind of travail to Hawthorne.   One must harpoon
him like a cetacean with questions to make him talk at all.
Then the words came from him at last, with bashful mani-
festations, like those of a young girl, almost, — words that
gasped themselves forth, seeming to leave a great deal more
behind them than they told, and died out, discontented with
themselves, like the monologue of thunder in the sky, which
always goes off mumbling and grumbling as if it had not
said half it wanted to, and meant to, and ought to say.

Emerson was sparing of words, but used them with great
precision and nicety.   If he had been followed about by a
short-hand writing Boswell, every sentence he ever uttered
might have been preserved.   To hear him talk was like
watching one crossing a brook on stepping-stones.   His
noun had to wait for its verb or its adjective until he was
ready; then his speech would come down upon the word
he wanted, and not Worcester and Webster could better it
from all the wealth of their huge vocabularies.

These are only slender rays of side-light on a personality
which is interesting in every aspect and will be fully illus-
trated by those who knew him best.   One glimpse of him
as a listener may be worth recalling.   He was always cour-
teous and bland to a remarkable degree ; his smile was the
well-remembered line of Terence written out in living features.   But when anything said specially interested him he

would lean toward the speaker with a look never to be forgotten, his head stretched forward, his shoulders raised like the wings of an eagle, and his eye watching the flight of the thought which had attracted his attention as if it were his prey to be seized in mid-air and carried up to his eyry.

To sum up briefly what would, as it seems to me, be the text to be unfolded in his biography, he was a man of excellent common-sense, with a genius so uncommon that he seemed like an exotic transplanted from some angelic nursery. His character was so blameless, so beautiful, that it was rather a standard to judge others by than to find a place for on the scale of comparison. Looking at life with the profoundest sense of its infinite significance, he was yet a cheerful optimist, almost too hopeful, peeping into every cradle to see if it did not hold a babe with the halo of a new Messiah about it. He enriched the treasure-house of literature, but, what was far more, he enlarged the boundaries of thought for the few that followed him and the many who never knew, and do not know to-day, what hand it was which took down their prison walls. He was a preacher who taught that the religion of humanity included both those of Palestine, nor those alone, and taught it with such consecrated lips that the narrowest bigot was ashamed to pray for him, as from a footstool nearer to the throne. " Hitch your wagon to a star;" this was his version of the divine lesson taught by that holy George Herbert whose words he loved. Give him whatever place belongs to him in our literature, in the literature of our language, of the world, but remember this: the end and aim of his being was to make truth lovely and manhood valorous, and to bring our daily life nearer and nearer to the eternal, immortal, invisible.

After the address of Dr. Holmes, the Rev. James Freeman Clarke, D. D., spoke of his long acquaintance with Mr. Emerson and read several interesting extracts from letters which he had received from him at an early period of his career. At the close of his remarks Dr. Clarke presented the following resolution, which was adopted by a rising vote : —

"*Resolved*, That this Society unites in the wide-spread expression of esteem, gratitude, and affectionate reverence paid to the memory of our late associate, Ralph Waldo Emerson, and recognizes the great influence exercised by his character and writings to elevate, purify, and quicken the thought of our time."

The following is a reprint, from the Proceedings of the Society, of the paper read by MR. EMERSON on the date and occasion above referred to : —

IMPRESSIONS OF THOMAS CARLYLE IN 1848.

THOMAS CARLYLE is an immense talker, as extraordinary in his conversation as in his writing, — I think even more so.

He is not mainly a scholar, like the most of my acquaintances, but a practical Scotchman, such as you would find in any saddler's or iron-dealer's shop, and then only accidentally, and by a surprising addition, the admirable scholar and writer he is. If you would know precisely how he talks, just suppose Hugh Whelan (the gardener) had found leisure enough in addition to all his daily work to read Plato and Shakespeare, Augustine and Calvin, and, remaining Hugh Whelan all the time, should talk scornfully of all this nonsense of books that he had been bothered with, and you shall have just the tone and talk and laughter of Carlyle.

I called him a trip-hammer with "an Æolian attachment." He has, too, the strong religious tinge you sometimes find in burly people. That, and all his qualities, have a certain virulence, coupled though it be in his case with the utmost impatience of Christendom and Jewdom and all existing presentments of the good old story. He talks like a very unhappy man, — profoundly solitary, displeased and hindered by all men and things about him, and, biding his time, meditating how to undermine and explode the whole world of nonsense which torments him. He is obviously greatly respected by all sorts of people, — understands his own value quite as well as Webster, of whom his behavior sometimes reminds me, — and can see society on his own terms.

And, though no mortal in America could pretend to talk with Carlyle, who is also as remarkable in England as the Tower of London, yet neither would he in any manner satisfy us (Americans) or begin to answer the questions which we ask. He is a very national figure, and would by no means bear transplantation. They keep Carlyle as a sort of portable cathedral-bell, which they like to produce in companies where he is unknown, and set a-swinging, to the surprise and consternation of all persons, bishops, courtiers, scholars, writers, and, as in companies here (in England) no man is named or introduced, great is the effect and great the inquiry. Forster of Rawdon described to me a dinner at the *table-d'hôte* of some provincial hotel where he carried Carlyle, and where an Irish canon had uttered something ; Carlyle began to talk, first to the waiters and then to the walls, and then, lastly, unmistakably to the priest, in a manner that frighted the whole company.

Young men, especially those holding liberal opinions, press to see him, but it strikes me like being hot to see the mathematical or Greek professor before they have got their lesson. It needs something more than a clean shirt and reading German to visit him. He treats them with contempt ; they profess freedom, and he stands for slavery ; they praise republics, and he likes the Russian Czar ; they admire Cobden and free trade, and he is a protectionist in political economy ; they will eat vegetables and drink water, and he is a Scotchman who thinks English national character has a pure enthusiasm for beef and mutton, describes with gusto the crowds of people who gaze at the sirloins in the dealer's shop-window, and even likes the Scotch nightcap ; they praise moral suasion ; he goes for murder, money, capital punishment, and other pretty abominations of English law. They wish freedom of the press, and he thinks the first thing he would do, if he got into Parliament, would be to turn out the reporters, and stop all manner of mischievous speaking to Buncombe and wind-bags. "In the Long Parliament," he says, "the only great Parliament, — they sat secret and silent, grave as an ecumenical council, and I know not what they would have done to anybody that had got in there, and attempted to tell out-of-doors what they did." They go for free institutions, for letting things alone, and only giving opportunity and motive to every man ; he for a stringent government that shows people what they must do, and makes them do it. "Here," he says, "the Parliament gathers up six millions of pounds every year, to give to the poor, and yet the people starve. I think if they would give it to me, to provide the poor with labor, and with authority to make them work, or shoot them, — and I to be hanged if I did not do it, — I could find them in plenty of Indian meal."

He throws himself readily on the other side. If you urge free trade, he remembers that every laborer is a monopolist. The navigation laws of England made its commerce. "St. John was insulted by the Dutch ; he came home, got the law passed that foreign vessels should pay high fees, and it cut the throat of the Dutch, and made the English trade." If you boast of the growth of the country, and show him the wonderful results of the census, he finds nothing so depressing as the sight of a great mob. He saw once, as he told me, three or four miles of human beings, and fancied that "the airth was some great cheese, and these were mites." If a Tory takes heart at his hatred of stump oratory and model republics, he replies, "Yes, the idea of a pig-headed soldier who will obey orders, and fire on his own father at the command of his officer, is a great comfort to the aristocratic mind." It is not so much that Carlyle cares for this or that dogma, as that he likes genuineness (the source of all strength) in his companions.

If a scholar goes into a camp of lumbermen or a gang of riggers, those men will quickly detect any fault of character. Nothing will pass with them but what is real and sound. So this man is a hammer that crushes mediocrity and pretension. He detects weakness on the instant, and touches it. He has a vivacious, aggressive temperament, and unimpressionable. The literary, the fashionable, the political man, each fresh from triumphs in his own sphere, comes eagerly to see this man, whose fun they have heartily enjoyed, sure of a welcome, and are struck with despair at the first onset. His firm, victorious, scoffing vituperation strikes them with chill and hesitation. His talk often reminds you of what was said of Johnson: " If his pistol missed fire he would knock you down with the butt-end."

Mere intellectual partisanship wearies him ; he detects in an instant if a man stands for any cause to which he is not born and organically committed. A natural defender of anything, a lover who will live and die for that which he speaks for, and who does not care for him, or for anything but his own business, — he respects : and the nobler this object, of course, the better. He hates a literary trifler, and if, after Guizot had been a tool of Louis Philippe for years, he is now to come and write essays on the character of Washington, on " The Beautiful," and on " Philosophy of History," he thinks that nothing.

Great is his reverence for realities, — for all such traits as spring from the intrinsic nature of the actor. He humors this into the idolatry of strength. A strong nature has a charm for him, previous, it would seem, to all inquiry whether the force be divine or diabolic. He preaches, as by cannonade, the doctrine that every noble nature was made by God, and contains, if savage passions, also fit checks and grand impulses, and, however extravagant, will keep its orbit and return from far.

Nor can that decorum which is the idol of the Englishman, and in attaining which the Englishman exceeds all nations, win from him any obeisance. He is eaten up with indignation against such as desire to make a fair show in the flesh.

Combined with this warfare on respectabilities, and, indeed, pointing all his satire, is the severity of his moral sentiment. In proportion to the peals of laughter amid which he strips the plumes of a pretender and shows the lean hypocrisy to every vantage of ridicule, does he worship whatever enthusiasm, fortitude, love, or other sign of a good nature is in a man.

There is nothing deeper in his constitution than his humor, than the considerate, condescending good-nature with which he looks at every object in existence, as a man might look at a mouse. He feels that the perfection of health is sportiveness, and will not look grave even at dulness or tragedy.

His guiding genius is his moral sense, his perception of the sole importance of truth and justice; but that is a truth of character, not of catechisms.

He says, " There is properly no religion in England. These idle nobles at Tattersall's, — there is no work or word of serious purpose in them ; they have this great lying church ; and life is a humbug." He prefers Cambridge to Oxford, but he thinks Oxford and Cambridge education indurates the young men, as the Styx hardened Achilles, so that when they come forth of them, they say, " Now we are proof : we have gone through all the degrees, and are case-hardened against the veracities of the Universe ; nor man nor God can penetrate us."

Wellington he respects as real and honest, and as having made up his mind, once for all, that he will not have to do with any kind of a lie.

Edwin Chadwick is one of his heroes, — who proposes to provide every house in London with pure water, sixty gallons to every head, at a penny a week ; and in the decay and downfall of all religions, Carlyle thinks that the only religious act which a man nowadays can securely perform is to wash himself well.

Of course the new French Revolution of 1848 was the best thing he had seen, and the teaching this great swindler, Louis Philippe, that there is a God's justice in the Universe, after all, was a great satisfaction. Czar Nicholas was his hero : for, in the ignominy of Europe, when all thrones fell like card-houses, and no man was found with conscience enough to fire a gun for his crown, but every one ran away in a *coucou*, with his head shaved, through the Barrière de Passy, one man remained who believed he was put there by God Almighty to govern his empire, and, by the help of God, had resolved to stand there.

He was very serious about the bad times ; he had seen this evil coming, but thought it would not come in his time. But now 't is coming, and the only good he sees in it is the visible appearance of the gods. He thinks it the only question for wise men, instead of art, and fine fancies, and poetry, and such things, — to address themselves to the problem of society. This confusion is the inevitable end of such falsehood and nonsense as they have been embroiled with.

Carlyle has, best of all men in England, kept the manly attitude in his time. He has stood for scholars, asking no scholar what he should say. Holding an honored place in the best society, he has stood for the people, for the Chartist,[1] for the pauper, intrepidly and scornfully teaching the nobles their peremptory duties.

His errors of opinion are as nothing in comparison with this merit, in my judgment. This *aplomb* cannot be mimicked ; it is the speaking to the heart of the thing. And in England, where the morgue of aristocracy has very slowly admitted scholars into society, — a very few houses only in the high circles being ever opened to them, — he has carried himself erect, made himself a power confessed by all men, and taught scholars their lofty duty. He never feared the face of man.

The following is the Speech by MR. EMERSON at the Burns Centenary, referred to by Mr. Hoar, in his letter as printed on a previous page : —

SPEECH BEFORE THE BOSTON BURNS CLUB.

MR. PRESIDENT AND GENTLEMEN,— I do not know by what untoward accident it has chanced — and I forbear to inquire — that, in this accomplished circle, it should fall to me, the worst Scotsman of all, to receive your commands, and at the latest hour, too,

[1] The Chartists were then preparing to go in a procession of 200,000, to carry their petition, embodying the six points of Chartism, to the House of Commons, on the 10th of April, 1848.

to respond to the sentiment just offered, and which indeed makes the occasion. But I am told there is no appeal, and I must trust to the inspiration of the theme to make a fitness which does not otherwise exist.

Yet, sir, I heartily feel the singular claims of the occasion. At the first announcement, from I know not whence, that the 25th of January was the hundredth anniversary of the birth of Robert Burns, a sudden consent warmed the great English race, in all its kingdoms, colonies, and states, all over the world, to keep the festival.

We are here to hold our parliament with love and poesy, as men were wont to do in the middle ages. Those famous parliaments might or might not have had more stateliness, and better singers than we — though that is yet to be known — but they could not have better reason.

I can only explain this singular unanimity in a race which rarely acts together, but rather after their watchword, each for himself — by the fact that Robert Burns, the poet of the middle class, represents in the mind of men to-day that great uprising of the middle class against the armed and privileged minorities — that uprising which worked politically in the American and French Revolutions, and which, not in governments so much as in education and in social order, has changed the face of the world.

In order for this destiny, his birth, breeding, and fortune were low. His organic sentiment was absolute independence, and resting, as it should, on a life of labor. No man existed who could look down on him. They that looked into his eyes saw that they might look down the sky as easily. His muse and teaching was common sense, joyful, aggressive, irresistible.

Not Latimer, not Luther, struck more telling blows against false theology than did this brave singer. The "Confession of Augsburg," the "Declaration of Independence," the French "Rights of Man," and the "Marseillaise" are not more weighty documents in the history of freedom than the songs of Burns. His satire has lost none of its edge. His musical arrows yet sing through the air.

8

He is so substantially a reformer, that I find his grand plain sense in close chain with the greatest masters — Rabelais, Shakespeare in comedy, Cervantes, Butler, and Burns. If I should add another name, I find it only in a living countryman of Burns. He is an exceptional genius. The people who care nothing for literature and poetry care for Burns. It was indifferent — they thought who saw him — whether he wrote verse or not ; he could have done anything else as well.

Yet how true a poet is he ! And the poet, too, of poor men, of hodden-gray, and the Guernsey-coat, and the blouse. He has given voice to all the experiences of common life ; he has endeared the farm-house and cottage, patches and poverty, beans and barley ; ale, the poor man's wine ; hardship, the fear of debt, the dear society of weans and wife, of brothers and sisters, proud of each other, knowing so few, and finding amends for want and obscurity in books and thought. What a love of nature ! and, shall I say it, of middle-class nature. Not great, like Goethe, in the stars, or like Byron on the ocean, or Moore in the luxurious East, but in the homely landscape which the poor see around them — bleak leagues of pasture and stubble, ice, and sleet, and rain, and snow-choked brooks ; birds, hares, field-mice, thistles, and heather, which he daily knew. How many " Bonny Doons," and " John Anderson my joes," and " Auld Lang Synes," all around the earth, have his verses been applied to ! And his love-songs still woo and melt the youths and maids ; the farm work, the country holiday, the fishing cobble, are still his debtors to-day.

And, as he was thus the poet of the poor, anxious, cheerful, working humanity, so had he the language of low life. He grew up in a rural district, speaking a *patois* unintelligible to all but natives, and he has made that Lowland Scotch a Doric dialect of fame. It is the only example in history of a language made classic by the genius of a single man. But more than this. He had that secret of genius to draw from the bottom of society the strength of its speech, and astonish the ears of the polite with these artless words, better than art, and filtered of all offence through his beauty. It seemed odious to Luther that the devil should have all the best tunes; he would bring them into the churches; and Burns knew how to take from fairs and gypsies, blacksmiths and drovers, the speech of the market and street, and clothe it with melody.

But I am detaining you too long. The memory of Burns — I am afraid heaven and earth have taken too good care of it, to leave us anything to say. The west winds are murmuring it. Open the windows behind you, and hearken for the incoming tide, what the waves say of it. The doves perching always on the eaves of the Stone Chapel opposite, may know something about it. Every name in broad Scotland keeps his fame bright. The memory of Burns — every man's, and boy's, and girl's head carries snatches of his songs, and can say them by heart, and, what is strangest of all, never learned them from a book, but from mouth to mouth. The wind whispers them, the birds whistle them, the corn, barley, and bulrushes hoarsely rustle them; nay, the music-boxes at Geneva are framed and toothed to play them; the hand-organs of the Savoyards in all cities repeat them, and the chimes of bells ring them in the spires. They are the property and the solace of mankind.

At the Commemorative recognition of Sir Walter Scott, as it was noticed by this Society, 15th August, 1871, MR. EMERSON spoke as follows : —

SIR WALTER SCOTT.

The memory of Sir Walter Scott is dear to this Society, of which he was for ten years an honorary member. If only as an eminent antiquary who has shed light on the history of Europe and of the English race, he had high claims to our regard. But to the rare tribute of a centennial anniversary of his birthday, which we gladly join with Scotland and indeed with Europe to

keep, he is not less entitled — perhaps he alone among the literary men of this century is entitled — by the exceptional debt
which all English-speaking men have gladly owed to his character
and genius. I think no modern writer has inspired his readers
with such affection to his own personality. I can well remember
as far back as when "The Lord of the Isles" was first republished
in Boston, in 1815, — my own and my schoolfellows' joy in the
book. "Marmion" and "The Lay" had gone before, but we
were then learning to spell. In the face of the later novels, we
still claim that his poetry is the delight of boys. But this means
that when we reopen these old books, we all consent to be boys
again. We tread over our youthful grounds with joy. Critics
have found them to be only rhymed prose. But I believe that
many of those who read them in youth, when, later, they come to
dismiss finally their school-days' library, will make some fond ex-
ception for Scott as for Byron.

It is easy to see the origin of his poems. His own ear had been
charmed by old ballads crooned by Scottish dames at firesides, and
written down from their lips by antiquaries; and, finding them
now outgrown and dishonored by the new culture, he attempted to
dignify and adapt them to the times in which he lived. Just so
much thought, so much picturesque detail in dialogue or description as the old ballad required, so much suppression of details, and
leaping to the event, he would keep and use, but without any am-
bition to write a high poem after a classic model. He made no
pretension to the lofty style of Spenser, or Milton, or Wordsworth.
Compared with their purified songs, — purified of all ephemeral
color or material, — his were *vers de société*. But he had the skill
proper to *vers de société*, — skill to fit his verse to his topic, and
not to write solemn pentameters alike on a hero or a spaniel. His
good sense probably elected the ballad, to make his audience larger.
He apprehended in advance the immense enlargement of the
reading public, which almost dates from the era of his books, — an
event which his books and Byron's inaugurated; and which,

though until then unheard of, has become familiar to the present time.

If the success of his poems, however large, was partial, that of his novels was complete. The tone of strength in "Waverley" at once announced the master, and was more than justified by the superior genius of the following romances, up to the "Bride of Lammermoor," which almost goes back to Æschylus, for a counterpart, as a painting of Fate, — leaving on every reader the impression of the highest and purest tragedy.

His power on the public mind rests on the singular union of two influences. By nature, by his reading and taste, an aristocrat, in a time and country which easily gave him that bias, he had the virtues and graces of that class, and by his eminent humanity and his love of labor escaped its harm. He saw in the English Church the symbol and seal of all social order ; in the historical aristocracy, the benefits to the state which Burke claimed for it; and in his own reading and research, such store of legend and renown as won his imagination to their cause. Not less his eminent humanity delighted in the sense and virtue and wit of the common people. In his own household and neighbors he found characters and pets of humble class, with whom he established the best relation, — small farmers and tradesmen, shepherds, fishermen, gypsies, peasant-girls, crones, — and came with these into real ties of mutual help and good-will. From these originals he drew so genially his Jeannie Deans, his Dinmonts and Edie Ochiltrees, Caleb Balderstone and Fairservice, Cuddie Headriggs, Dominies, Meg Merrilies and Jeannie Rintherouts, full of life and reality ; making these, too, the pivots on which the plots of his stories turn ; and meantime without one word of brag of this discernment, — nay, this extreme sympathy reaching down to every beggar and beggar's dog, and horse and cow. In the number and variety of his characters, he approaches Shakespeare. Other painters in verse or prose have thrown into literature a few type-figures, as Cervantes, DeFoe, Richardson, Goldsmith, Sterne, and Fielding ; but Scott portrayed with equal strength and success every figure in his crowded company.

His strong good sense saved him from the faults and foibles incident to poets, — from nervous egotism, sham modesty, or jealousy. He played ever a manly part. With such a fortune and such a genius, we should look to see what heavy toll the Fates took of him, as of Rousseau or Voltaire, of Swift or Byron. But no : he had no insanity, or vice, or blemish. He was a thoroughly upright, wise, and great-hearted man, equal to whatever event or fortune should try him. Disasters only drove him to immense exertion. What an ornament and safeguard is humor! Far better than wit for a poet and writer. It is a genius itself, and so defends from the insanities.

Under what rare conjunction of stars was this man born, that, wherever he lived, he found superior men, passed all his life in the best company, and still found himself the best of the best! He was apprenticed at Edinburgh to a Writer to the Signet, and became a Writer to the Signet, and found himself in his youth and manhood and age in the society of Mackintosh, Horner, Jeffrey, Playfair, Dugald Stewart, Sydney Smith, Leslie, Sir William Hamilton, Wilson, Hogg, De Quincey, — to name only some of his literary neighbors.

www.ingramcontent.com/pod-product-compliance
Lightning Source LLC
Chambersburg PA
CBHW030717110426
42739CB00030B/713